A Move in the Weather

GW00724747

Anthony Thwaite

A Move in the Weather

Poems 1994–2002

ENITHARMON PRESS

First published in 2003
by the Enitharmon Press
26B Caversham Road
London NW5 2DU

www.enitharmon.co.uk

Distributed in the UK by
Central Books
99 Wallis Road
London E9 5LN

Distributed in the USA and Canada
by Dufour Editions Inc.
PO Box 7, Chester Springs
PA 19425, USA

ISBN 1 900564 58 0 (paperback)
ISBN 1 900564 84 X (hardback)

The hardback edition, bound by The Fine Bindery,
is limited to thirty signed and numbered copies, each one
containing a handwritten poem from the collection.

British Library Cataloguing-in-Publication Data.
A catalogue record for this book is available
from the British Library.

Typeset in Bembo by Servis Filmsetting Ltd
and printed in England by
Antony Rowe Ltd

CONTENTS

ACKNOWLEDGEMENTS

Several of these poems first appeared in the following periodicals and anthologies: *Illuminations* (U.S.A.), *London Magazine*, *New Writing 10* (Picador, for British Council), *Poetry Review*, *The Rialto*, *The Shop*, *Sightlines* (Vintage, for R.N.I.B.), *Spectator*, *Sunday Times*, *Times Literary Supplement*. Eighteen of them were first collected in a limited edition, *A Different Country* (Enitharmon Press, 2000).

for Ann

In 1936

'*Sabbat-Goy: a gentile hired by Jews*
To carry out the Sabbath household tasks
Which their religion forbids them to perform.'

★

It was in Leeds in 1936,
In Roman Terrace, by our red-brick house.
I stood there with a boy, who said to me:

'That house just opposite — take care
You don't walk near it on a Saturday.
They're Jews, and they might grab you, make you cook

Their dinner for them.' I didn't ask him why.
I couldn't even boil an egg. At six years old
What did I know of *Jews*, even the word?

Now, sixty-four years later, I remember
That mystery, that warning; and remember
Ariadne Rothstein, the strange

Name of my friend at school, with frizzy hair,
I hugged and kissed and (so I'm told) once bit
In an excess of friendship. It was 1936.

In the barber's chair in Hathersage
I forgot who I was. The summer of '39.
Heat in the hedges among the butterflies.

Looked back on now as I move into old age,
That terror too comes back, as I sit, aged nine,
In the barber's chair and feel the heat rise

From the tangle of hedges outside, my body, my head
Buzzing and helpless under the clippers, fear
Blanking me out as I lose identity.

It was as if I was already dead,
No longer anywhere, not even here
Wherever I am, silently screaming 'Me!'

They had their mountains, frontiers, capitals,
Principal products, rivers, forests, lakes,
But most of all they had their armies, each
Regiment numbered, each with uniforms
Distinct, badges of rank, precise gazettes
Of infantry, artillery, and names
Of generals and commanders. Behind these
Were lists of cabinet-appointments, dates
Assigned to revolutions, executions,
The histories that these two countries had.

And when was this? The years before the War,
When I was eight and coming up to nine.
They were my countries, safe inside my head
But needing this enumeration, dreams
Enacted in these drawings, maps, lists, all
The imagined stuff I had to get correct.
Dreary compulsions, maybe: not to me,
Who wanted them to make sense of a world
In which I stood poised on the very edge
Of unimagined things that soon were true.

Next door was empty, and the next-door yard
Was overgrown with flowers floating high
In tangles among weeds, where wild things stirred
That were not weeds: lizard, butterfly,
Cicada, mantis, big-horned bug. At night
The firefly blinked its hot excited light.

Sub-tropical suburban paradise,
That long-baked summer set me there transfixed,
And everything was fire as sharp as ice,
The new and recognised blindingly mixed.
A scarlet cardinal bubbled and flew by,
Huge turkey-buzzards drifted in the sky.

And I was there alone, all of it mine
To linger in away from everything,
To count each mottled brilliance, each pronged spine,
Distinctions on the palette of each wing.
Day after day the next-door yard lay there
To drug me with its jungle-laden air.

It was America, and I was ten.
The place was commonplace: I did not know.
I try to bring it back as it was then,
Try to make present what was long ago.
But it won't come to me, that wilderness
Next to an empty house, an emptiness.

Dredging through all these folders, papers, files,
Meticulous accounts, the scurf of money
Long spent, my mother's reading-lists, things any
Archivist might properly sort out,
I plan to bin the lot, a bonfire's-worth of blaze.
I should have done all this a year ago,
After her death, twenty years after his,
But sifted through, uncertain.
                              Till these fragile pages came
Into my hands, a sheaf of typescripts, all
The poems that my father wrote that year
In 1941 – all the poems
He ever wrote, that year of war, while I was far away
Safe in America. Later, he said
They coincided with a TB spot
Found on his lung, and doctors blotted out:
As if, at thirty-eight, the romantic blight
Forced him to write them.
                              No, they're not much good,
Bits of Masefield, Belloc, Chesterton,
Or wistful Georgian lyricism, like the stuff
He used to quote to my embarrassment
When I was nine, and hated poetry –
Turned, in these poems of his, to simulacra,
Desperate gestures, quietly discreet,
Unlike the man I knew, my father, faint
Pastiches lingering on and out of sight.
And yet they speak to me, tell me much more
Than I can cope with in this silt of mess.
They must be saved, and handed on. The fire
Eats up the accounts, the lists, and all the rest.
These faded yearnings will evade the flames.

Down to the tiny harbour,
The western edge of the peninsula:
Five herons chevroned in a tall pine tree
Fly off and suddenly let loose the rain,
Drenching the landscape till we only see
An umbrella's distance beyond the pure stain
Of the liner lying there on the jetty's edge –
That white perfection, with its brass plate clear –
Stella Polaris.
                    The name rings to me
Across the decades, the same ship that bore
Me off to Norway, 1947.

The symmetry of ships, chaos of seventeen.

It was the same ship, built in '27,
A vessel for a millionaire, transformed
To pleasure-liner, and finally to this
Moored relic in Japan, by chance found
Here in the tiny harbour in the rain.

What happened there, fifty-four years ago,
That cynical seduction by suave 'Maurice'
(So eager to hear my adolescent lusts
Rehearsed until he took me like a fish)
Turned me to stone, to liquid, swept me back
Against the breakers to another shore.

Back to the jetty, then, my own old self,
The temple at the harbour-entrance, where
Five herons left the pine tree empty, rain
Shuddered in sheets, and where
Chrysanthemums scattered on the cypress floor.

BOHEMIA

Lifting a half of bitter in Fore Street
In the company of the poet and printer Guido Morris
And the painter Sven Berlin, with intimate talk
Of the absent poets Barker, Graham, Wright,
I visit for the first time those fabled shores.

I had met these luminaries in the second-hand bookshop
Run by two willowy brothers who spoke in code
Of all these exalted beings, artists who clung
To the rungs of fame with no visible support
Except that passport to my yearned-for country.

St Ives, Cornwall, is the real place.
I am eighteen, on holiday this Easter
Before the army claims me. Mother and father
Are there, and pay for it; but are not there
In the pub in Fore Street with my new-found friends.

Fifty years later, I read of Guido Morris,
Who died, unknown, as a London Underground guard;
Of Sven Berlin, who ended up in the gutter.
I went to another place, a different country.
I have never since visited Bohemia.

A sack of straw suspended from a frame,
And six of us lined up with 303s
Extended with our bayonets held at ease
Until the brisk sergeant-instructor came
And told us what to do and how to do it.

Advance – in, out, in, out, twist, and pull clear –
And then advance again. The straw sack swung
This way and that, and that shrill raucous tongue
Lashed us for feebleness, for sloth, for fear:
'You *hate* the bastard – *show* him how much'. The sun

Shone down on Hampshire hills, and our platoon
Formed and re-formed and did it all again.
Ten thousand miles away, other young men
Would do the same in earnest, very soon,
Told what to do, and doing it, and dying.

A place where every dune is topped with stone,
Dressed stone brought low and littered on the sand,
Where shifting winds reveal these scattered sherds
And in whose acres you must be alone.
There in the heat you stand
In a lost landscape, and are lost for words.

This is the place you know, or think you know,
From times when you were young, or thought you were.
It will not go away. It stays with you
In dreams and daydreams. And it will be so
In that far landscape where
There will be nothing left of what you knew.

ARCHAEOLOGY

How would it be if we remembered nothing
Except the garbage and the rubbishing,
The takeaways, the throwaways, the takeovers,
The flakes and breakups, the disjected members
Scattered across the landscape, across everything?

Nothing stands up, nothing stands clear and whole,
Everything bits and pieces, all gone stale,
All to the tip, the midden topped up high
With what we used, with what we threw away:
How would it be if this was all we could feel?

That will not be. Remembering, or feeling,
Or knowing anything of anything,
Will be the last we know of all this stuff.
It will be there for others, seekers of
Things that remain of us, who then are nothing.

They move so solidly across this space –
He curls his left arm round her willing dress
From which one breast breaks loose; and his right hand
Twiddles a sword that could be something else.

In front of them, an interrupted drunk
Spews copiously, hands held above his head,
Helpless and knock-kneed, while his wife looks back,
Her face obliterated with disgust, or age.

Uncertain, on the left – a man, maybe,
Lurching towards them: to the right, another
Arm intervenes, curtailed. Above, below,
Words run in strips, clumsy, reversed, obscure.

In stiff and fixed licentiousness, around
And yet around, though broken to a sherd
Jagged and arbitrary, all that's left
Of prancing peasantry, stamped with two big initials –

IE – Jan Emens: and a neater date –
One five seven six. The crafty potter caught
By name, in time, four centuries ago,
And more. The figures move, and dance – quick quick quick, slow.

A Bib of Lace of the late Queen's Maid of Honour.
A little fragment of an Indian's skin.
Some Chinese engines made to ease the Ague.
Some feathers from an Angel in a Tree.
A Nun's long stockings worn for Chastity.
A mummied Rat from an Egyptian Tomb.
A gut-stone passed by a hanged Sodomite.
Another Stone formed like an ancient Worm.
A great Bird's beak, too large for a living bird.
A painted ribbon from Jerusalem
With which our Blessèd Saviour was bound
To the Temple's pillar when He was crowned and scourged.
An Instrument for measuring the wind.
A Vase of glass to hold a Roman's tears.

LATE

Late in learning how to tie my tie,
To know my tables, boil a kettle, drive a car,
Now I have come this far
To face new skills I can't begin to try:
Ways to employ a mouse, or pay a visit
To websites full of dots, or drill my fingers
To log into a message-board. What is it
That makes me tardy, clumsy?
                        What is it lingers?
Have I come all this way to know no more
Than what I learned so late and long before?

They are arguing about money in the hotel bar
In a foreign country about which they know nothing
Except they are short of it, and feel cheated.
They have maybe been married a long long time,
So long they feel in a foreign country and feel cheated
Of everything except they know each other much too well
To argue about anything except money.
They are on holiday. The holiday will soon be over.
And yet they go on arguing about money in the hotel bar
In a foreign country about which they know nothing.

Catching the train that day, there opposite
Was Imogen Holst, by chance, recognised
Quite how I don't know. Laid out between us
Sheets of music paper, all the lines and notes
Under her quick bright eye and poised pen
Held almost like a baton.
I could just make out, on the top margin, the name –
Gustav – upside down. What she was up to
I was ignorant of, dear devoted daughter
Making her stabbing, almost nervous marks.

But as we approached London
After those hours of fixed concentration,
She looked up, caught my gaze, and a great smile
Irradiated her small neat serious face;
And in my inner ear there soared that tune
Pulsing through Jupiter, the bringer of joy.

Now it comes back, twenty-two years ago;
The name, the place, where I was asked to go –
Middle of nowhere, further off from Moscow
Than London was from Moscow, to a name
That sounded like a parody of itself:
Novosibirsk.

And 'British Week'. A flight of 'experts' (art,
Industrial design, geology,
Music – a Scottish bagpiper'd been hired
By Caledonian Airways – fashion, science)
Flew, and I with them: 'British Poetry'.

What stays, then, what comes back?
                                    A concrete wedge,
The Union Hall of some official sludge,
In which this Cultural Festival took place.
Endless reshufflings of the rubric planned –
I made unwise remarks on censorship
Before the censor intervened: a band
Of mufti secret-police stood, with each face
Bewilderingly the same. And then came on
A gorgeous troupe of local models, clad
In all the latest London rag-trade stuff,
And Solzhenitsyn was forgotten.

                                    Britten
Was briskly done by some well-skilled quartet;
And so to dinner, vodka-toasts before
Numbered on the fingers of two hands.
Companion on my left, an Irish violin
Who slumped into his soup; and on my right
A fluent speaker of American
I took to be our minder, KGB.

Emboldened with potato-spirits, I
Took up my set of freedom-cudgels, leant
Towards this smoothy, and spelt out my spiel –
Why did this vast and powerful panoply
Bother about a few stray 'dissidents'?
He inclined towards me, gazed into the air,
And told me this: 'Ah, Mr Thwaite, you err
In your imagined notion of our strength.
We are not strong: our East and South are full
Of Muslimites who breed unheedingly
Like rabbits, and they know their time will come,
When they will overthrow us. We must keep
Vigilance, always, against these Asian hordes,
Though they pretend they're Soviets, like the rest.
Let one speak out, the others will join in,
Our whole great enterprise collapse and die.'

Next morning, an unscheduled trip downtown:
One stop, a bookshop, with another hood
In charge of us – until he had to go
On some more urgent business. At once
Customers moved towards us, whispering,
Asking us questions suddenly and fast,
Telling us things we almost dared not hear.
It did not last long. We were whisked away,
On to another numb 'exchange of views'.

And then the model schools, Akademgorodok,
Where some of us were drafted in to judge
The language-skills – and plausibility –
Of white-bloused boys and girls arranged in rows
To speak their English to us for a prize.
Each question brought a prim and ready answer,
Mouthed prettily, and clearly learned by heart,
And recitations, Shakespeare, Byron, Scott –
'My heart's in the Highlands, my heart is not here' –

Until that twelve-year-old who faced us down
With hesitances that seemed all his own,
A boy who knew his mind in that charade:
'I think that Byron was not true with women'.
We gave the prize to him. He went away,
But never took it up – the foreign trip
Our rules insisted. He returned to school
And did not come to England: 'Security'
Forbade it.

    Then we flew back. Moscow Airport,
Some bother over forms not signed on entry,
Some bureaucratic blunder – tired with this,
I pressed ahead beyond the barrier,
To be met by some grey-clad tough with a grey gun:
I gently pushed him to one side, and went
Onto the tarmac. Later, I realised
The folly and the danger. But we flew
Out of Great Russia, far from Novosibirsk,
Safely to London; middle of nowhere, never
Ever again the same. Siberia.

THROES

Being with her now is a kind of boredom,
A dullness in which guilt and pain both ache,
When all my childish anguish after freedom
Has long since vanished. Now I wait to take

Her back to her own loneliness, where she
Can follow boredom of a different kind,
Routine quite unresented, and set free
From all required constraints. She is resigned,

Stoic and still, to what is left to come:
First blindness, then a sequence no one knows –
Choked lungs, paralysis, delirium?
Each one may follow where the other goes.

We act out cheerfulness to one another,
Exchanging memories, recalling names:
Son in his sixties, ninety-year-old mother,
Playing our boring, life-sustaining games.

Old mothers, their time running out, when time doesn't matter,
Keep on consulting their watches, as if puzzled how time
Runs on, even when
Meals arrive on time, and each day a different carer
Arrives and takes over:
Even then
They look at their watches again and again and again.

Again and again and again they look at their watches,
As if puzzled how time runs on and on and on
Even when meals arrive
On time, and each day a different one
Arrives and is eaten:
Still alive,
Old mothers, when time doesn't matter, time running out.

The worst words, the words that hurt,
Are the words you don't use.
You are afraid to use them, because they hurt
And you know they will hurt.

So you go on using another sort of words.
They are the words that please, or at least get by.
They make life easier, they grease the wheels,
And no one notices them as they go by.

Until there comes a moment when the worst words
Are the ones you need, the words to do the trick,
The worst trick, to tell the terrible truth.
But it is too late. You have lost the trick of those words.

THE MESSAGE

I keep it in my pocket, take it out,
Read it again, then put it back, this scrap
Of envelope with those scratched and blurred
And urgent words I found stuffed in your bag –
A cry of rage, of misery, of mad
Incomprehension, just
Enough like your familiar hand to stun
The one you wrote it to: your son.

Now I have read the words so many times
I know them all by heart; but can't repeat
Or spell them out in my own writing. Grief
Blanks out their meaning, as your stroke blanked out
Whatever happened, and whatever followed.
I take the paper out and follow it
Again, once more, its deadened, endless shout:
Why have you done this to me? Take me out.

Not dead, not dead yet –
Like a cry curtailed
The words come back to me, and in her voice.
And it is terror that I feel at this
Impossible coming-back, the future filled
With that unstoppable presence night by night.

And yet I know she's dead, and wanted it
As I too wanted it. Why should she cry
Like this, persistent ghost
Asking to be missed
So strongly, plaintively, and nightly?
Not dead, not dead yet.

'Would you let a crack of air in' – as I tucked
Your small frail body into bed
That early night, a week before you died,
You spoke those words I hear and recollect
Again and yet again.
They seemed like hope renewed, as if pain
Might still be turned away
By letting freshness in, till a new day
Brought light through opened windows, and the sun
Rose in its old way.

But that was habit speaking. You were old
And tired and far beyond a crack of air,
Or light, or anything to hold
The darkness back in bed as you lay there.

Pressed to remember her, I dredge up stuff –
Such stuff, unwilling bits of this and that,
Trivia unearthed, washed clean in fragments, dumped
Into a letter to have done with it.

When did I meet her? Where? Forty-two years
Lie heavy on the page: I can't recall
The words we spoke, but glumly paraphrase
What passed between us, things he wants me to tell

To help with his 'research'. Out of it all
Emerge the outlines of too many facts,
No substance, flavour, colour. Somewhere else
The things that go beyond 'the poet's texts'.

Most things that happen mean nothing at all to us:
This is known as being oblivious.

STROKE

'I always seem to cry', he said, and tears
Stood in his eyes as if confirming this
Admission of whatever had gone wrong:
A switch thrown back; a failure in the brain;
Close-down of numbers, names; a cave of fears
Echoing mixed unspeakable menaces,
And the same thing said again and again and again.

He lay there with the others in the ward –
Others plugged in to this and that device
Constructed for emergencies not his.
They were all silent. He at least could speak.
But words were useless tokens of regard,
Shapes he could make with lips, but not entice
Sense from the cave with tears, dumb, fearful, weak.

For Edwin Brock: 1927–1997

A voice I'd never try to emulate –
Now there's a word you'd never ever use,
Edwin, south London sniffing out the false:
'Emulate' – academic Latinate,
A vocable you'd smile at, and say 'crap'.

And yet you waded through long years of crap,
Agency-talk which you turned into gold,
Campaigns and slogans and the selling phrase
Your colleagues envied. If it was a trap
You slipped out of the cage, always ran free.

You ran into the arms of someone free
To share those thirty years you had ahead:
After the mess of childhood, blue tattoos
That marked you out in some lost atrophy,
You sailed into the meadows of content.

I think of you smiling, benign, content,
And now I see you – as I often do –
Pushing a wheelbarrow, trimming a tree,
Putting a not-quite-finished poem through
Our letterbox: one I could never emulate.

Out of that mess of relatives you came,
A breathless blonde, a giggling saboteur,
Silly, subversive, resolute, and clever.
You mocked, and flirted, and you had no shame.

I felt uneasy with you, always did:
You puffed out put-downs with your nicotine.
You made me think of what I might have been.
And then you made this last intricate bid –

A book on breaking-out, on making-out,
Through all those years of stress and mess, 'bad blood'
Fed through your veins, until you gasped and stood
Triumphant there, there on the last redoubt.

RELICT

(Monica Jones: d. 2001)

Propped up among pillows and ruins of pillows,
Chin jutting out from an eiderdown furrowed by books,
The bedside table littered with bottles and glasses,
Confronting the world with one of your famous looks,
Your enormous spectacles bright under grease-plaited hair,
And the bedroom shrunk to that drunk, spectacular stare.

He had brought you here, in a terror of love and despair,
Both selfish, knowing you sick. He tried to be fair.
Both of you nibbled at snacks, and drank, looking at books,
While the days and the months went by. And now it passes –
Forty years and more, together, with him dead, and your looks
Lurk among heaped-up pillows and ruins of pillows.

St Mary's, Wimbledon

(for Ian Hamilton)

Your few remains,
Tight-reined, tight-lipped,
Remain. My parodies
(Those hands, that hair,
Those brief intensities)
You grimly smiled at, knowing
What I was getting at: the stripped
And naked things no one but you could do
And others only copied.
Now there is nothing here
In the packed church you'd not have visited
Unless in this sealed lid,
Except old thickened friends,
White-haired, with slowing pulse,
Our ageing hands
Handing you on to somewhere, somewhere else.

In this dream, a rope or ropeway rises up,
Up a steep slope ahead. Things like bobbins loop
The rope between them. I am somewhere there,
But somehow distant in the foggy air
And terrified. The whole thing scales the sky
Out of my sight, beyond my lost body
Packed in the crevices of ice and stone:
And here I lie, and here I am alone,
As the thick cords rise above
The things that hold them, shuddering to move
Whatever it is they carry.

Down in the valley
An expedition gathers to explore
A far-off moraine on the glacier
Where they will find this body packed in ice,
Sealed in the snowfalls of the centuries,
And heave it out, and label every bone
Each bound to each,
Then carry everything stitch by stitch
Down to the base-camp – the rope disappeared,
The fog around the bobbins cleared,
Only this body there,
Which seems my body in the pure bright air.

Have you noticed,
Approaching the cashpoint machine, your card at the ready,
Another standing there at his quiet business
And behind that person another?
The one who stands behind averts his attention
From the one who does business.
And you, the third in transaction, hold back a little
Behind your forerunner, as he behind this one who frowns
Over the aperture in front of him.

How silent it all is,
Much like the orderly manner of men who wait
In the urinal on a different business:
The reluctance to speak as the indifferent machines
Perform at a slight distance, extracting, discharging.

Alex is almost four, and knows ways to behave.
'Being silly' is not one of them.
He knows his Grandpa shouldn't be like this.

Kicking my feet up, pulling a face,
Putting on funny voices – this is 'being silly',
And Alex hates it, wants to tell me so.

So he takes his Grann off, and says to her:
'Please let me talk to Grandpa by myself'.
He tells me what he has to say. I promise.

And so I am not silly. I know how to behave,
At least in front of Alex. How to behave
Elsewhere is something I have still to learn.

THE HALL OF HOLY RELICS

Here is the Hall of Holy Relics
to which the Faithful make their Pilgrimages
now that the Public is allowed to see them.

Here is the Saucepan of Prophet Ibrahim,
the Baton of Prophet Moses, the Sword of Prophet David,
the Cap of Prophet Yusuf.

Here is the Description of Prophet Mohamed on a Copper Plate,
the Tooth, broken, of Prophet Mohamed,
three Footprints in Marble of Prophet Mohamed
all different in size, each a Miracle.

Here is the Famous Cloak bestowed by Prophet Mohamed
on a Poet who submitted to the Will of Allah,
and here is the Letter sent by Prophet Mohamed
with an Embassy to the Copts of Egypt
threatening the worst if they did not submit to the Will of Allah.

Here is the Dust brought from the Tomb of Holy Prophet
    Mohamed,
and here the Photo of the Document citing the Dust
brought from the Tomb of Holy Prophet Mohamed.

★

In the Chambers where helwa and various syrups were made
various glasswares are now displayed.

★

This is a Blasphemous Poem by a Christian dog
who thinks he can sneer because he has a different God.

★

He is mistaken. Wrath will descend on him.
The Hall of Holy Relics will extinguish him.

Names

(for Ortwin de Graef)

The Buenos Aires telephone directory:
Benito Takahashi, Ricardo Jones,
Moelwyn Rodrigues, Hanan Fricasee.
They hide behind their hidden telephones.

Japanese-Tuscan, Cymric-Lebanese,
Polyglot fore- and surnames on each page,
Do they spell out profuse misceganies
Or just the casual mixings of the age?

To ask this is a dubious business, true.
Septimius Severus, with his Punic burr,
Escaped such censure by being someone who
Adopted names which would avoid the slur

Of acting Emperor under alien guise:
He took protective colouring, and shed
African origins. And this proved wise.
When he lay sick in York, and then was dead,

He handed on the imperial sobriquet.
It is not thus with those who still bear here
Misnomers of a more plebeian day.
Their names may carry stigma, and they fear

Questions upon the road: 'Seamus?', 'Othman?'
Somewhere in Kosovo, or Lebanon,
These are presented. In victory or defeat,
At Belfast checkpoints, in a Bosnian street,

Your mother's name, or patronymic, blur
Into a confrontation, insult, threat.
You answer to your name. And some infer
It smells of ancient, hostile matters yet.

The gorse pods explode under the sun
Strewn on the chalk hump of the down
Where at another time there stalked tall Tennyson,

Muttering into his cloak, with his hat pulled down,
Looking daggers at anyone or no one,
Breathing his sixpenny pints of air under the sun.

And now there is no one there, or anyone,
Just his tall memorial Celtic cross on top of the down
As the gorse pods explode like the mutters of Tennyson.

My poor old tired eyes –
I catch a headline, and it says
ANTHONY THWAITE:
My paranoia surfaces, and then
I see, though dimly, the true phrase –
ANTHRAX THREAT. Since when
The world seems safer, at least to my eyes.

JOURNEY

Overtaken on a blind corner by an empty hearse,
She wondered whether anything could be worse
Than being smashed up by a van that had shed a corpse
Or was on its way to find one.
                                 She slowed down,
Gathered her faculties, let her worries lapse.

So she drove on, with meticulous care, to the town
Where she was due to book in for three days
Of chemotherapy, hairless, in a gown
That shrouded her from the world's insulting gaze.

It was a dead time. Ice on the river,
Snow on the banks, snow on the far field,
Sky white to the top, trees bare.

And nothing moved. Stiffly, the landscape held
Steady as rock, steadier than ice. The wind
Had dropped into a wide unmoving stare.

Till something moved: a thing with wings came down
Looking for something there, whatever it was.
There on the snow a brilliant patch, a stain

Concentrated, and still. And there it lies,
One spot of colour, gathered, focused, where
Whatever happened happened. What it was

Disturbs the landscape, hides itself away.
It is as if some angel in the air
Came to its aim on the appointed day

And touched the other's tongue with a cinder of dead fire.

Yesterday, half a Saxon glass bead
In a field at Shotesham.
Today, a pound in the gutter in Long Stratton.

Waiting all day for six o'clock:
My first cigarette.
Such will-power. Such weakness.

Hearing a grandchild's voice
In the night: is it my child
From forty years ago?

Reading these old cuttings
Does nothing but tell me how
Somehow I wrote them once.

Deciding not to write
An obituary of my friend
Even before he dies.

Today, I put off again
Something which yesterday
Was all I had to do.

Trying to put into words
My objection to four words:
'And also with you'.

'Vain repetitions' – a phrase,
However archaic,
Both solemn and exact.

'Never again', she said
Over and over again.
Thus remarked, again and again.

The cloud of unknowing
Never far away
From the fog of ignorance.

THE SUMERIAN ANTHOLOGY

(for John Mole)

First we must put in Ur
Because he began everything:
Everyone knows that.

Then decent representation
Of Enki, Enlil, Nannar –
Try to include some less obvious pieces.

The early stuff of Uruk, that elegy
By Eridu, at least something
By Lagash before he dried up.

So far, easy. But approach the present –
What about Kul, Dhrondro, Salugi,
Nobut, Luth . . . ? Difficult to sort out:

They look a bit arbitrary. Well,
Pick one by each of them. Make sure
The headnotes balance respect with limiting judgements.

It will all be the same in five thousand years.

THE ART OF POETRY:
TWO LESSONS

i

Write in short sentences. Avoid
Unnecessary breaks. Strictly control
(Or totally eliminate) the adverb.
Eschew such words as 'myriad'. Adopt
Current demotic, yet be wary of
Brand-names, and proper-names
Limited by time. The Latinate
Is out, except for satire.
Ease yourself into the vernacular.
If you are male, try to forget the fact:
If female, use the fact as document –
It will allow you entry as yourself.

These are beginnings: when you have begun,
Forget the lot, and try to swim alone.

ii

Travel. Hot countries. Half an anecdote,
The other half left to imagined things.
Of these you will not speak. Strew here and there
Stray relatives – your people people poems.
In the alembic, scatter something rough,
Not easily digested. Let the mix
Come to the boil, cool off.
Hint urgency, but not in too much a hurry.

All these are precepts, and not recipes.
Whoever lays down laws lays down his head
On reputation's stiff, objecting block.

The aspirant asks, 'Why, if these things are so,
Have you not done them?' And I reply,
'The very fact you ask will tell you why'.

UNTITLED

Sometimes you want to tell everything –
Not all in a rush, but plain and full and true,
And all in good time: everything you knew
And all you have always known, telling
All, without qualification,
Without explanation.

What holds you back, then, from this great recital,
This major melody, this noble strain?
Ah, that is what you never can explain:
You know how it goes, you even know the title,
But the act of making
Is an act of breaking.

TUNE

Humming and ha-ing to a tune in the head
Not knowing whatever it is that lies up ahead
But going on strumming away at whatever it may be
It sits deep inside like an egg or a baby.

Don't try to push it too hard or it may drop away
Like a dinosaur's coprolite fossilised in the clay,
Or a light that is quenched, or a drink that has sunk too far,
Or a star out of sight, or a shape beyond reach of radar.

Nothing will tell you when the right time has come
Tapping and titupping on its hesitant drum.
You will know when it happens. You may know what it means.
But nothing shows clear on the murk of the blurred screens,

Till the word trips up, and the trap trips over, and then
The sounds rebound and the voice begins again,
Dictating the straight sense you know you knew
And the humming and ha-ing tune in to the new, the true.

MAJOR POEM

This is the big one for the end of time
Which will survive the end of time:
Not yet written but as good as written
If I can get it right.

This is what I am about to write,
Something that will never be forgotten
Even when there is no idea of time
Or very little time.

Well, he just fell apart. Nothing dramatic
But bits of him from time to time fell off.
At first we didn't notice, nor did he,
We think, because each bit was so minute:
A comb of hairs, a rind of skin, a scar,
Until the squabble turned into a war,
A battle of attrition. What was static
Went mobile when a tickle changed to cough,
An itch became a furnace, suddenly
He was a duck-pond with a shark in it.
The cough erupted, and the itch exploded,
The shark smelt blood, tore the whole thing apart.
We noticed then, at last; though whether he did
We don't know. What we're left with is his heart.

So much is so easy, a current that flows as it goes
Over its long smooth bed, between reeds that bend
Unhindering anything, under a wind
That blows in the way things go, on to the end
Where rivers descend to the easy beckoning seas.

So much is so hard, a push up a bend that sticks
With a clutter of mud meshed hard against banks that jut
Congested with logs that lash together and get
Plaited with clay and stick like a stuffed gut
That rids itself of nothing, can never relax.

FOR KETTLE

Poor old creature, friend for eighteen years,
Your spine and ribs too sharp, your cry so quiet,
You lie disconsolate, and bring to mind
The lion of St Jerome in that altar-piece,
The saint's companion in this passing world,
Who now lies miserably curled
At the side of the bed which has just become a bier:
As if in dumb reaction to the grief
Others more piously indicate above
With praying hands, letting a devout tear
Drop in the margin of this Pietà,
You and that big cat behave
With weary instinct, imitate with grace
Something we want somehow to mark as love.

First it was wilderness. Then it was cut down,
Tamed and settled. Now wilderness again.
Here and there, distant, a small town
But thickening forests between.

There they are now, in the heat of late afternoon,
Dense screens of green, with the creek and the pond between
Grumbling with bullfrogs, and three deer suddenly seen
On the edge of a meadow which almost becomes a lawn.

Beyond that clearing, rank upon rank of trees
Slip into solid blurs, as dense as night.
The heat unravels in the evening breeze
Gathering far shudders of smudged light.

So from the porch, the past moves under my eyes
Without a meaning, and without a cause,
And the mist from the tall hills and down in the valleys
Hovers over it all. So it is, and was.

'Spirit birds': 'Skins'

Sunk deep in yellow jars, they lie
Still as aborted babies, still
With stiffened sodden wings. They fill
Shelf after shelf, thrust long ago
Into their spirit flasks. To fly
Is far beyond, behind them. Go
Along the shelves, behind the screens,
And find them labelled one by one –
Century-stained identities
Meticulously written down,
Preserved: what each one was and is
Fixed in nomenclature, specimens.

Then to another corridor,
Similar, dark as theirs, you see
Another kind of history:
The coloured plumages are bright
As those that in their lives they wore –
Crimsons, fierce yellows, blues the light
You bring them into fleshes out.
These are the skins, the feathered pelts
Of birds collected as these were
But chosen to lie differently.
The others' meaning, sealed, now melts
Into a vacuum, vacancy.
Those, loose, transcend their vanished species.
They too lie still; but, as they lie,
Their wings almost begin to fly
Again, their hues alert and bright,
Their dry inertness poised for flight
Flashing beyond the window's present light.

SAINT'S DAY, CARDOSO

They bicker in the square in celebration
Of the saint whose day it is, as voices rise
And butt against the bells, as candles run
Across and pour in each piazza, as the day's
End flows down the mountain in its floods
Of heat and mist and silence through their words.

And we are silent here who hear such things
Late in the late afternoon, come drowsy back
From a long lunch across the bridge. Hot wings
Bear up flown creamy clouds, blown thick
With sun and saturation, clefts and trees,
The river's drought, rocks spilling down the valleys.

The saint's one day evaporates in ritual:
He is carried here and there in delicate balance,
And the swifts fall and rise, rise and fall,
Above these annual urgings towards reverence,
Then glide away towards the sky's dark edge
Where there are no words; no piazza; mountain; bridge.

To the Waterfall

(for Ronald Ewart)

Walking again the track to the waterfall
Twenty years after, same heat, same smell,
Blown from late summer, and still

The sullen shade that shakes down from the trees:
Remembering this walk is not what it says
Now. It has become its memories:

Dogs scampering ahead, and children's voices,
And sudden laughter in high picnic places,
All shaken into far too many pieces.

But that is not it, either. All that air,
All those sounds and stones and leaves, nowhere
Except where they gather here –

Particular, different, not to be expressed
Distinctly, vague as the mist
Down in the valley below, a vast

Diffusion of each step we chose to take
Time and again, as those leaves unshook
Year after year, walking along that track.

SYRIA

At every intersection, in each square,
Stone superman, bronze bust, or smiling father
Ride above traffic-fret gigantically.

They promise force, and fear, and permanence,
They warn and chasten, clenched in one strong man.
They stand unshaken and invincibly.

★

South of Aleppo blow the plastic bags:
Tatters of polythene in thornbushes,
The desert wind shredding them fitfully.

These stunted leafless junipers, festooned
With such parodic fluttering foliage,
Quiver and jerk and twitch continually.

All other rubbish rusts, rots, vanishes
Along the dunes among the dusty trees.
Only these remnants last perpetually.

There in the background are the soldiers,
Helmeted, pikes held ready,
One looking on intently
At the stooped offerings presented,
The big black chieftain standing to the side.
Someone is muttering in Joseph's ear.

Those unimportant onlookers Bruegel put there
Are Spanish. They are the occupying power,
Distrusted, loathed, alien.
And they are there because the message is
Even the enemy must come to this
Moment when God arrived to save all men.

'Perched like an eagle' (in the guide-book phrase),
Five thousand feet up, pocked with caves and graves
Packed into scoured-out rock, where the defile
Slices its course through channels long run dry
Except this trickle turning dust to mud,
The mountain gives way to this orifice.

Inside the chapel, an oval granite womb,
Sounds from outside are muffled, or distorted,
Or shrunk to nothing. We shed our shoes, go soft
On long-rubbed stone. The light reflects bright ikons
Littered along the rock-face, kaleidoscope
Of gaudy golds and crimsons, saints and halos.

All this exotica, in this tourist-trap,
Plucks at me fitfully, almost resented –
A pointless pilgrimage. Till suddenly
A girl's pure voice utters alien words,
Those Aramaic cadences that begin
'Abba', flow on, as if known, to 'Amen'.

In this dry place my eyelids fill with tears.

Maalula, Syria

These old arcane contritions, ancient sounds
Compounded of such alien traditions –
Shinto, Judaic, Syriac, Hindu – thread
Beseeching wails with solemn ululations
Over the holy places, over the buried dead.
Canticle, veda, sutra, chant their still
Archaic keening among the killing grounds,
The darkness into which their pure sounds spill.

Something to do with love, with grief, with death,
All share this common melody, ascend
And fall and rise again, repeat again
Cadences that return, that never end
Until the melisma of extended pain
Shudders and drops in wordless stubborn stress
With resignation, with exhausted breath,
Over the risen hope, over the hopelessness.

MOVEMENTS

As ice keeps the shape of the bowl
after the bowl is broken,
and the pad in the mud is sure of the bird's sign,
and the bruise on the skin is taken
as a mark of the blood underneath troubled and shaken,
so is the shape of the invisible soul.

As the current wavers and suddenly changes,
plucked by the wind, which no one has ever seen,
and leaves shaken above turn again and again
from white, then to grey, to black, to green,
and their branches fret above from now to then,
so the door between *then* and *now* shifts on its hinges.

As the mist in the headlights lifts and comes down again,
marking a move in the weather we did not know,
and the river rises with only a flurry of snow
melting under a warmth we could not see,
nothing is sure, nothing can ever stay,
so much is the one thing sure, as sure now as then.